Taylor Swift

BY JODY JENSEN SHAFFER

Published by The Child's World®
1980 Lookout Drive • Mankato, MN 56003-1705
800-599-READ • www.childsworld.com

Acknowledgments
The Child's World®: Mary Berendes, Publishing Director
The Design Lab: Cover and interior design
Amnet: Cover and interior production
Red Line Editorial: Editorial direction

Photo credits
Amy Nichole Harris/Shutterstock Images, cover, 1; Pat Bonish/
Bigstock, 5; Seth Poppel/Yearbook Library, 7, 8, 11; Mark J.
Terrill/AP Images, 13; Judy Kennamer/Shutterstock Images, 14;
Mark Humphrey/AP Images, 17; Debby Wong/Shutterstock
Images, 19, 22; Helga Esteb/Shutterstock Images, 21; Charles
Sykes/AP Images, 24, 29; Shutterstock Images, 27

Design elements
Sergey Shvedov/iStockphoto

ISBN 9781614732976
LCCN 2012933738

Printed in the United States of America
Mankato, Minnesota
July 2012
PA02128

Table of Contents

CHAPTER 1

A Shooting Star

It only took a few years for Taylor Swift to make her mark on the country music world. She began as an unknown singer-songwriter. But three years after releasing her first single, Taylor was named country music's Entertainer of the Year. She beat out longtime country stars such as George Strait and Kenny Chesney.

Taylor's rapid rise began in 2006. That is when the then 16-year-old released the single "Tim McGraw." It became the lead title on her first album, *Taylor Swift*.

Taylor said she wrote "Tim McGraw" during her freshman year of high school. "I got the idea in math class," she said. "I was just sitting there, and I started humming this melody."

Taylor Swift sings at a 2009 concert in Wyoming.

Five songs from that album made the country top-ten list. Taylor became the youngest person to write and sing a number-one country single, "Our Song." *Taylor Swift* had sold more than 3.5 million copies through 2011.

CHAPTER 2

Early Life

Taylor Alison Swift was born on December 13, 1989. Her hometown is Wyomissing, Pennsylvania. Taylor's father, Scott, ran a Christmas tree farm. He also sold **stocks** part-time. Meanwhile, Taylor's mother, Andrea, stayed home and cared for the house. Taylor has a younger brother named Austin.

Taylor had a happy childhood. She went to school, rode horses, played soccer, and sang to the music of Disney movies. She could remember all the lyrics. Taylor's mom encouraged Taylor to do outdoor activities.

In fourth grade, Taylor won a national poetry contest. Her three-page poem was called "Monster in My Closet."

Taylor was interested in poetry
and music while attending high school.

Taylor performs a song while in high school.

Taylor went to school in Pottstown, Pennsylvania. She loved to read and write poetry. She read books by Dr. Seuss and Shel Silverstein. Once, Taylor's fourth-grade class was assigned to write a poem. Some of her classmates complained. Taylor rose to the challenge.

Taylor said poetry sparked her interest in words and in writing. "Poetry is what turned me into a songwriter," she said. Taylor's favorite themes for her songs and poems are romance, love, and heartbreak.

CHAPTER 3

Singing and Acting

Taylor began singing in local contests and festivals at age ten. Her grandmother, Marjorie Finlay, was an **opera** singer. "I can remember her singing, the thrill of it," Taylor said. "She was one of my first inspirations."

Taylor wanted to sing in front of bigger crowds. She knew sporting events often drew big crowds. And each sporting event begins with a song! So Taylor began singing the national anthem at sporting events beginning at age 11. Some were big events. Among them were a Philadelphia 76ers basketball game and the US Open tennis tournament. However, Taylor also sang at local garden parties.

Taylor also loved to act. She performed with a children's acting company between the ages of ten and 12. Taylor was tall and could play adult parts. That helped her often get the **lead role**. Taylor played Sandy in *Grease*, Kim in *Bye, Bye Birdie*, and Maria in *The Sound of Music*.

Taylor enjoyed acting in plays. She also enjoyed the parties that took place afterward. That was where she discovered the **karaoke** machine. Taylor sang songs by the Dixie Chicks, Shania Twain, and Faith Hill. People who heard Taylor sing said she should take up singing as a job.

Taylor is 5 feet 11 inches (1.80 m) tall!

Taylor sings a song while in high school in Pottstown, Pennsylvania.

CHAPTER 4

Emerging Artist

Taylor grew up in Pennsylvania. However, she knew the country music capital of the world was farther south, in Nashville, Tennessee. At age 11, Taylor begged her mom to take her there on a trip. Taylor quickly got to work once she arrived.

Taylor went to the offices of several **record labels**. She left them copies of her karaoke tapes. None of those labels asked Taylor to make an album with them. But Taylor did not give up her dream of singing country music.

Taylor had an unexpected first guitar lesson. Her first teacher was a man her parents hired to fix their computer.

Taylor began playing guitar while in middle school.

Not everybody at Taylor's middle school liked country music. Some of her classmates made fun of Taylor for liking it. So Taylor began writing her feelings in a diary. She also began learning how to play guitar.

Nashville, Tennessee, is known as the capital of country music.

Taylor began entering a local karaoke contest. The winner would perform before a famous country singer at a concert. Taylor performed in the contest for more than a year. Finally, she won. Taylor got to open for Charlie Daniels. He is a popular country musician and fiddle player.

Taylor's family was excited by her success. So her parents decided to move the family to Hendersonville, Tennessee. It was about 20 miles (32.2 km) from Nashville. Taylor was just 14 years old. But she wanted to be close to the music world. Her parents knew she had the drive and the talent to succeed.

Taylor considers 13 to be her lucky number.

CHAPTER 5

Career in High Gear

At 13, Taylor had signed a deal with RCA Records to be a songwriter. But she was unhappy with that setup. Taylor wanted to sing her songs as well as write them. So she left RCA a year later. Record deals are very hard to get. It is very uncommon for an unknown musician to walk away from one.

The decision worked out for Taylor. In May 2005, Sony/ATV hired Taylor as a staff songwriter. At age 15, she was the youngest person ever hired for that job. While Taylor wrote songs, she continued singing wherever she could.

Record **producer** Scott Borchetta heard Taylor singing once at the Bluebird Café. He was impressed.

Taylor poses with her guitar in 2006.

Borchetta signed her to Big Machine Records. Her first song was "Tim McGraw." It launched her music career during the summer of 2006. She cowrote the song with Liz Rose.

Her first album was *Taylor Swift*. It was released in 2006. Taylor wrote or cowrote all the songs. "Tim McGraw" was its lead track. Tim McGraw is a famous country singer. The album did well. However, Taylor continued singing the national anthem at sporting events. She also sang at restaurants. Then her album took hold. *Taylor Swift* had sold 3.5 million copies through 2011.

Taylor left high school for her junior and senior years to focus on her work. She was homeschooled. Taylor earned straight As.

Taylor plays an outdoor concert for her adoring fans.

CHAPTER 6

Awards and Appearances

Taylor began writing songs for her next album, *Fearless*. She also released a Christmas album in 2007. It was called *Sounds of the Season: The Taylor Swift Holiday Collection*. Country music organizations began taking notice of Taylor. The Academy of Country Music named Taylor the Top New Female Vocalist. Country Music Television (CMT) also awarded her the Breakthrough Video of the Year for "Tim McGraw."

Taylor got big news in 2008. That was the year she was named a finalist for a Best New Artist Grammy. The Grammy Awards are perhaps the most respected in the music industry. Taylor lost to

Taylor has won several awards for her music.

Taylor performs a song during a live television show.

Amy Winehouse. But just being up for the award was a big honor for the 19-year-old.

Around that time, Taylor also began appearing on magazine covers such as *USA Weekend* and *People*. She also released a shorter album called *Beautiful Eyes* later in 2008. And she sang the national anthem at game three of the World Series.

Taylor's next album, *Fearless*, was released in November 2008. It **debuted** at number one on the Billboard 200 albums chart and shattered sales records.

In 2009, Taylor performed on the television show *Saturday Night Live*. She also appeared on the television show *CSI: Crime Scene Investigation*.

Taylor won several awards for her music videos. MTV honored her at the Video Music Awards. Taylor won the Best Female Video award. She was unable to accept her award, though. Rapper Kanye West stormed the stage as Taylor was talking. He took the microphone from her and argued that Beyoncé deserved to win. Later, Beyoncé won the award for Video of the Year. She called Taylor to the stage to finish her acceptance speech. West later apologized to Taylor. Still, many people were upset with West. They sided with Taylor, and she became even more popular.

Taylor had a number-one hit from her *Fearless* album called "Love Story." Taylor told *Time* magazine she spent just 20 minutes writing it on her bedroom floor.

Taylor sometimes has fireworks at her concerts.

Broadcast Music, Inc. (BMI) named Taylor's song "Love Story" as the Song of the Year in 2009. She also swept the Country Music Awards that year. Taylor won awards for the top Female Vocalist, Album, and Music Video. She was also named Entertainer of the Year. Taylor became the youngest person ever to win the last award.

In 2009, Taylor went on a 52-city tour through the United States and Canada. Tickets for her show in Los Angeles, California, sold out in two minutes.

Taylor wrote songs for the movie *Valentine's Day*. She also acted in that movie. In addition, Taylor was named a CoverGirl spokesperson. She also appeared on many television shows.

Taylor released her third album, *Speak Now*, in October 2010. She wrote all the songs. They had themes similar to her previous songs. Many were about love, heartbreak, and romance. By August 2011, the album had sold more than 5.5 million copies.

In October 2011, Taylor said she did not have a boyfriend. However, she has been linked romantically to musician Joe Jonas and actors Jake Gyllenhaal and Taylor Lautner.

Taylor developed her own perfume in 2011. It was called Wonderstruck. She also voiced the role of Audrey in the animated film *The Lorax*. It was released in early 2012.

CHAPTER 7

A Good Girl

Sometimes people who gain fame begin to act out. After all, with fame often comes lots of money and opportunities. Many people want to be associated with stardom. However, Taylor has not given in to the **temptations**.

Taylor is known as a good girl. She told *Rolling Stone* magazine that she has never smoked a cigarette or taken a drink of alcohol. "I have no interest in drinking," she said. "I always want to be responsible for the things I say and do."

In September 2010, Taylor donated $75,000 to her old high school in Tennessee. The money went to improve the sound and lighting system in the school's auditorium. The high school renamed the auditorium in Taylor's name.

Taylor signs autographs for some fans.

Some of Taylor's biggest fans are teenage girls. Many parents like Taylor, too. They like that she is a good role model in addition to being a good musician.

CHAPTER 8

The Future

Taylor once said she "never felt like the coolest girl in the room. Ever." Many of her fans would disagree. With hard work, Taylor made herself into a country music star as a teenager. And she appears to be just getting started.

Taylor had plans to release a fourth album in 2012. She also planned to continue touring around the world and possibly do more acting. And it is on those tours where she writes some of her favorite music. "I do love writing on the road . . . I'll find a quiet place in some room at the venue, like the locker room," she said.

Whatever the future holds for Taylor, she is sure to make the most of it. Taylor knows how to succeed. "To succeed in life," she said, "it takes ignoring so many people who tell you it's not possible."

Taylor sings at a concert in New York City.

GLOSSARY

debuted (day-BYOOD): Something debuted when it appeared for the first time. Taylor's album debuted at number one.

karaoke (kar-ee-OH-kee): Karaoke is a song somebody sings over accompanying music. Taylor got her start singing karaoke.

lead role (LEAD rohl): The actor who plays the main character has the lead role in a production. Taylor had the lead role in many musicals.

opera (AH-pur-uh): Opera is a style of musical in which the words are sung in a certain way. Taylor's grandmother was an opera singer.

producer (pruh-DOOS-ur): A producer finds the money to make an album and supervises its production. Taylor works with a producer when recording music.

record labels (REK-urd LAY-bul): Record labels are companies that manufacture, distribute, and promote audio and video recordings. RCA Records and Sony/ATV are record labels.

stocks (STAHKS): Stocks are individual shares of something, such as a company. Taylor's dad sold stocks for a living.

temptations (temp-TAY-shuhns): Temptations are bad things that people desire. With fame often comes temptations.

FURTHER INFORMATION

BOOKS

Bloom, Ronny. *Get the Scoop: Taylor Swift*. New York: Price Stern Sloan, 2009.

Linde, Barbara M. *Taylor Swift*. New York: Gareth Stevens, 2011.

Peppas, Lynn. *Taylor Swift (Superstars)*. New York: Crabtree Publishing Company, 2010.

WEB SITES

Visit our Web site for links about Taylor Swift: **childsworld.com/links**

Note to Parents, Teachers, and Librarians: We routinely verify our Web links to make sure they are safe and active sites. So encourage your readers to check them out!

INDEX

ABOUT THE AUTHOR

Jody Jensen Shaffer is a poet and the author of several books for children. She writes from the home she shares with her husband, two kids, and dog in Missouri.